BEI GRIN MACHT SICH IHR WISSEN BEZAHLT

- Wir veröffentlichen Ihre Hausarbeit, Bachelor- und Masterarbeit

- Ihr eigenes eBook und Buch - weltweit in allen wichtigen Shops

- Verdienen Sie an jedem Verkauf

Jetzt bei www.GRIN.com hochladen und kostenlos publizieren

Bibliografische Information der Deutschen Nationalbibliothek:

Die Deutsche Bibliothek verzeichnet diese Publikation in der Deutschen National-bibliografie; detaillierte bibliografische Daten sind im Internet über http://dnb.d-nb.de/ abrufbar.

Dieses Werk sowie alle darin enthaltenen einzelnen Beiträge und Abbildungen sind urheberrechtlich geschützt. Jede Verwertung, die nicht ausdrücklich vom Urheberrechtsschutz zugelassen ist, bedarf der vorherigen Zustimmung des Verlages. Das gilt insbesondere für Vervielfältigungen, Bearbeitungen, Übersetzungen, Mikroverfilmungen, Auswertungen durch Datenbanken und für die Einspeicherung und Verarbeitung in elektronische Systeme. Alle Rechte, auch die des auszugsweisen Nachdrucks, der fotomechanischen Wiedergabe (einschließlich Mikrokopie) sowie der Auswertung durch Datenbanken oder ähnliche Einrichtungen, vorbehalten.

Impressum:

Copyright © 2016 GRIN Verlag, Open Publishing GmbH
Druck und Bindung: Books on Demand GmbH, Norderstedt Germany
ISBN: 9783668264465

Dieses Buch bei GRIN:

http://www.grin.com/de/e-book/323151/simulating-routing-protocols-between-two-university-campuses-to-replicate

Kagiso Andy Malepe

Simulating routing protocols between two university campuses to replicate a video conference application

GRIN Verlag

GRIN - Your knowledge has value

Der GRIN Verlag publiziert seit 1998 wissenschaftliche Arbeiten von Studenten, Hochschullehrern und anderen Akademikern als eBook und gedrucktes Buch. Die Verlagswebsite www.grin.com ist die ideale Plattform zur Veröffentlichung von Hausarbeiten, Abschlussarbeiten, wissenschaftlichen Aufsätzen, Dissertationen und Fachbüchern.

Besuchen Sie uns im Internet:

http://www.grin.com/

http://www.facebook.com/grincom

http://www.twitter.com/grin_com

DTech. Computer Systems Engineering
Systems Simulations 4

Simulating routing protocols between CPUT campuses

Written by:

Kagiso Malepe

Academic Year: 2015-2016

Index

1.　　　Abstract

In this modern age where everything depends on the internet, the importance of using available network resources to our advantage efficiently especially routing packets is starting to be appreciated. Routers are an essential part of the rapid growth of the internet and in the general networking community.

Routers mainly direct packets or messages to a desired destination using routing protocols and transport protocols. It is important for one to configure their router using the most appropriate routing protocol to suit their needs.

In this study, traffic was generated to replicate a video conference application and simulate routing protocols between routers representing virtual CPUT campuses.

2.   Aims and objectives

The aim of this project is to study the functionality of Routing Information Protocol (RIP) and Open-shortest Path First (OSPF) and determine which of the two takes the least amount of time to route packets from a source to a destination.
Objectives:

- Create subnets in a network
- Simulate routing protocols on routers
- Generate virtual traffic.

3.   Introduction

3.1. Video

Video can be described in different forms, namely; streaming, pre-recorded, low resolution, high resolution, conferencing etc. For the purpose of this simulation, video conferencing was the main focus.

A video is a sequence of images played at a certain interval/ rate and the images are commonly known as frames. Frame rate is directly proportional to resolution which is a measure of pixels in an image. A greater frame size generally equates to better video quality. Video has a lot of standards which affect the quality of the video including aspect ratio, audio, codecs, etc, and these values are used to calculate frame rate.

$$Frame\,rate = (Resolution \times Bit\,rate)/(Bytes \times Kilobytes)$$

3.1.1. Video Conferencing

Video conferencing is a technology that allows two or more people to have a live video call over the internet usually in a business setting. Any smart device with a microphone and a camera can essentially be used to conduct a video conference call.

There are different video and audio compression formats and codecs (coder/ decoder) are used by devices to solve this issue during a video call. The most common video codec is H.264 which is used in high definition systems such as Blu-ray, HDTV and popular video-sharing websites such as Vimeo and YouTube.

The tables below indicate typical frame rates and total frame sizes which are found in videos coded by the H.264 codec. (Coded 2003)

6 fps	12 fps	25 fps
• local stores • single-family homes • offices • housing developments • playgrounds	• warehouses, stockrooms • production facilities • large stores • parking lots • areas with moderate traffic	• train, bus etc. stations • stadiums • concert halls • discos • cities • areas with dense traffic

Frames per second to bits per second

Resolution	25 fps	12 fps	6 fps
1080p (1920x1080)	3 Mbps - 9 Mbps 32-10 days	4096 kbps 23 days	3072 kbps 31 days
UXGA (1600x1200)	3 Mbps - 9 Mbps 32-10 days	4096 kbps 23 days	3072 kbps 31 days
720P (1280x720)	2.5 Mbps - 6 Mbps 47-16 days	1792 kbps 54 days	1536 kbps 63 days

3.1.2. Transmission Control Protocol (TCP) and User Datagram Protocol (UDP)

TCP is a transport protocol used to transport packets from a source to a destination. TCP ensures a reliable same order delivery to a destination when packets are sent in a stream. TCP has error detection methods, and recovery mechanisms to ensure reliability. TCP is mostly used in applications where it is critical for the recipient to receive data exactly as it was sent without any errors or parts of the data missing. Although this method ensures complete packets and reliability, it can however cause long delays.

UDP is also a transport protocol which transports packets from a source to a destination except it ensures a faster track transport mechanism unlike TCP. The main disadvantage with UDP is that packets cannot be tracked or recovered when there was a loss of packet, meaning there is no way of knowing whether the message was delivered or not. UDP is commonly used in real-time systems such as live video streams, VoIP, etc. or applications where time is crucial and users want to send as much data as possible within a specific amount of time.

3.2. Routing protocols

Routing protocols are router based protocols where routers share routing tables and use algorithms to determine a best route to a destination. There are multiple types of routing protocols such as RIP, OSPF, EIGRP, BGP, ISIS, etc. In this study, only RIP and OSPF are simulated since they the most commonly used.

3.2.1. RIP (Routing Information Protocol)

RIP is a hop-count based routing protocol which is commonly used in non-complex networking environments to transfer datagrams from hosts to destinations. RIP is only limited to 15 hops and can count source to destination metrics up to infinity. However, RIP is not suitable for real-time applications because counting metrics such as delays can take time when dealing with several hundreds of interconnected networks.

3.2.2. OSPF (Open - shortest Path First)

OSPF is a link-state routing protocol which uses routing tables to calculate the shortest route or path to a destination. OSPF connects to other routers (also called areas) securely with a password authenticated method to keep a record of their links state. OSPF is the most commonly used internet routing protocol compared to RIP and IGRP

3.3. Network metrics

3.3.1 End-to-end delay

The end-to-end delay is the time it takes to transfer a packet from one node to another (source/ destination). The end-to-end delay is affected by a couple of factors namely; transmission delay, which is the time taken to transmit a packet from a host to an outgoing link (the first encountered router), propagation delay which is the speed at which a packet travels and is dependent on the packet length, and lastly queueing delay which is the time it takes a node to wait for previous jobs to complete before sending a new packet.

3.3.2. Jitter

The variation of delay between packet round-trip time where the time it takes for packets to be sent to a destination is not the equal to the time at which the source received packets. Jitter is commonly used at a metric to weigh a network's strength.

3.3.3. Bandwidth

Bandwidth is the rate at which bits are received or sent between nodes. It is commonly known as the network speed by the public and to be the one factor which determines how fast or slow a network operates. Bandwidth is measured in bits per second(bps).

3.4. Networking tools

3.4.1. Graphical Network Simulator (GNS3)

GNS3 is a Cisco software which allows users to simulate virtual network environments on Cisco routers. GNS3 runs on Dynamips, which is the main program which takes care of all the necessary nuts and bolts to essentially imitate a real live network infrastructure. Big organizations such as Hewlett Packard (HP), NASA and IBM use GNS3 to test all their infrastructure before testing on physical hardware.

GNS3 utilizes Internetwork Operating Systems (IOS) images which represent different versions and models of routers. GNS3 IOS images generally run on virtual machines.

3.4.2. Wireshark

Wireshark is a packet sniffer and analyser tool. It is mainly used to inspect which packets are sent to which nodes and through which protocol and also solve network problems. Wireshark has the ability to sniff any interface (lan, wlan, bluetooth, etc.) on a device and store all the packet information sent over a network in a capture file.

3.4.3. Internet Protocol Service Level Agreement (IP SLA)

IP SLA is a Cisco based IOS tool used to monitor applications at a system level and network performance on nodes in real-time. Apart from monitoring networks, IP SLA could also be used to generate traffic for UDP, TCP, ICMP, HTTP, DNS, etc. between a source and a destination. Variable such as frequency, packet size, time-outs, etc. could all be configured.

3.5. Network topologies

Network topology describes the arrangement of devices or nodes in a network (Pandya 2013). There are multiple types of network topologies including mesh, star, tree, etc. Each topology is arranged as the name suggests and the mesh topology is the only one used in this project.

3.5.1. Mesh topology

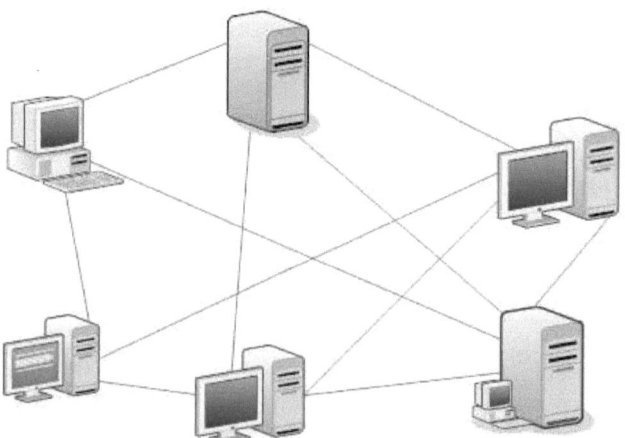

In a mesh topology, all devices are connected to each other, as in the image above. This setup increases security and privacy of messages between devices which makes the topology more robust. The main advantage of this topology is that there are multiple routes to each device, meaning that an alternative route is always available when there is a broken connection in any of the networks.

3.6. Subnet Masking

As we know that each node gets assigned a unique ip-address which uniquely identifies nodes connected together in the same network. Subnet masking plays a vital role when it comes to dividing a single network into multiple, smaller networks which could/ could not have access to each other depending on the desired configuration by an administrator. This helps on reducing load on a network since each subnet has a minimal amount of hosts. In subnet rules, the first ip-address is always reserved as the network gateway and the last ip-address as the broadcast ip-address.

The table below represents an example of subnets and their ranges. (Humphrey, 2016)

Net bits	Addresses	Hosts	Net mask	Amount of a Class C
/30	4	2	255.255.255.252	1/64
/29	8	6	255.255.255.248	1/32
/28	16	14	255.255.255.240	1/16
/27	32	30	255.255.255.224	1/8
/26	64	62	255.255.255.192	1/4
/25	128	126	255.255.255.128	1/2
/24	256	254	255.255.255.0	1
/23	512	510	255.255.254.0	2
/22	1024	1022	255.255.252.0	4
/21	2048	2046	255.255.248.0	8
/20	4096	4094	255.255.240.0	16
/19	8192	8190	255.255.224.0	32
/18	16384	16382	255.255.192.0	64
/17	32768	32766	255.255.128.0	128
/16	65536	65534	255.255.0.0	256

4.   Methodology

4.1. Network Topology

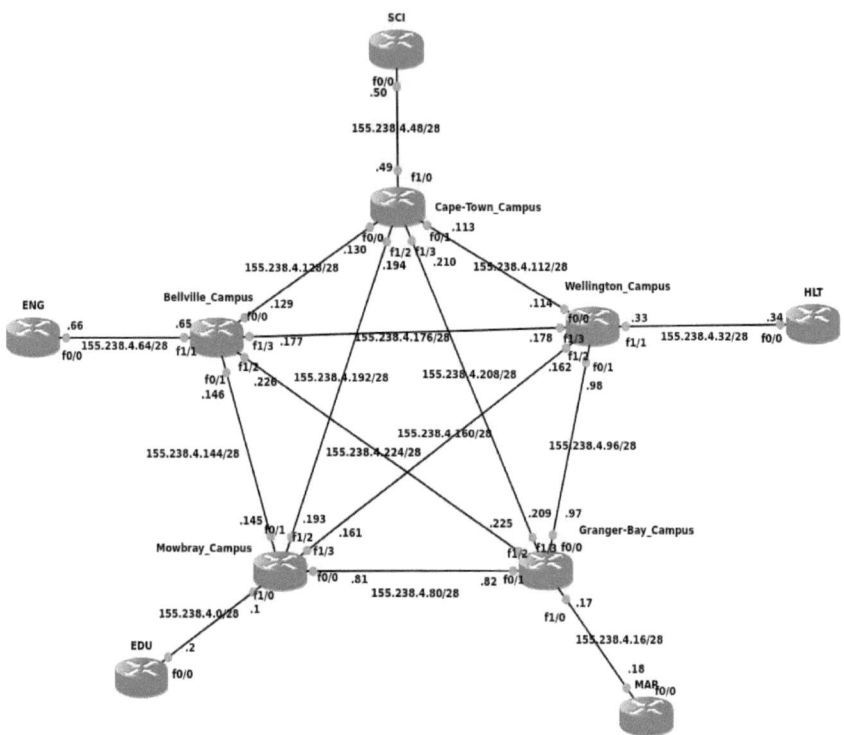

Figure 3.1.   CPUT campuses

Five main routers representing CPUT campuses were connected through fast-ethernet ports in a mesh topology created in GNS3. Each port was assigned a static a ip-address through a console. A *ping* was executed to test communication among routers.

4.2. Subnets

Using the formula, $2^n = Number\ of\ subnets$ where n is the binary position number, 16 networks were created but only 15 were used with each network being capable of having 13 hosts.

As in binary numbers:

1	1	1	1	1	1	1	1
128	64	32	16	8	4	2	1

11111111.11111111.11111111.11110000

255 . 255 . 255 . 240

ip-address used for subnets: 155.238.4.0

Subnet mask: 255.255.255.240

List of networks:

155.238.4.0/28,	155.238.4.16/28,	155.238.4.32/28,	155.238.4.48/28,
155.238.4.64/28,	55.238.4.80/28,	155.238.4.96/28,	155.238.4.112/28,
155.238.4.128/28,	155.238.4.144/28,	155.238.4.160/28,	155.238.4.176/28,
155.238.4.192/28,	155.238.4.208/28,	155.238.4.224/28,	155.238.4.240/28

4.3. Commands to assigning ip-address to interfaces

The commands below are an illustration of how one the interfaces belonging to the Mowbray_Campus' router was assigned a static ip address.

enable   #enable router

configure terminal   #enter into configuration mode

interface f1/0   # select interface: interface <interface>

ip address 155.238.4.1 255.255.255.240   #ip address <ip-address> <subnet mask>

no shutdown

interface f1/2

ip address 155.238.4.193 255.255.255.240

no shutdown   #keep router in an up-state

interface f1/3

ip address 155.238.4.161 255.255.255.240

no shutdown

interface f0/1

ip address 155.238.4.145 255.255.255.240

no shutdown

interface f0/0

ip address 155.238.4.81 255.255.255.240

no shutdown

exit

4.3.1. Verifying ip-addresses configuration

show ip route

Sample output:

155.238.0.0/28 is subnetted, 9 subnets

C	*155.238.4.80 is directly connected, FastEthernet0/0*
R	*155.238.4.64 [120/1] via 155.238.4.146, 00:00:09, FastEthernet0/1*
C	*155.238.4.0 is directly connected, FastEthernet1/0*
R	*155.238.4.224 [120/1] via 155.238.4.146, 00:00:09, FastEthernet0/1*
C	*155.238.4.192 is directly connected, FastEthernet1/2*
R	*155.238.4.176 [120/1] via 155.238.4.146, 00:00:09, FastEthernet0/1*
C	*155.238.4.160 is directly connected, FastEthernet1/3*
C	*155.238.4.144 is directly connected, FastEthernet0/1*
R	*155.238.4.128 [120/1] via 155.238.4.146, 00:00:10, FastEthernet0/1*

4.4. Commands to configuring RIP on router

enable

configure terminal

router rip   #configure RIP on router

network 155.238.4.1   #add connected networks; network <network>

network 155.238.4.80

network 155.238.4.192

network 155.238.4.160

network 155.238.4.144

end

4.4.1. Verifying routing protocol configuration
show ip protocols

Sample output:

Routing Protocol is "rip"

  Outgoing update filter list for all interfaces is not set

  Incoming update filter list for all interfaces is not set

  Sending updates every 30 seconds, next due in 26 seconds

  Invalid after 180 seconds, hold down 180, flushed after 240

  Redistributing: rip

  Default version control: send version 1, receive any version

Interface	Send	Recv	Triggered RIP	Key-chain
FastEthernet0/0	*1*	*1 2*		
FastEthernet0/1	*1*	*1 2*		
FastEthernet1/0	*1*	*1 2*		
FastEthernet1/2	*1*	*1 2*		
FastEthernet1/3	*1*	*1 2*		

  Automatic network summarization is in effect

  Maximum path: 4

  Routing for Networks:

  155.238.0.0

  Routing Information Sources:

Gateway	Distance	Last Update
155.238.4.146	*120*	*00:00:21*

  Distance: (default is 120)

4.5.   Commands to configure OSPF on router
enable

configure terminal

router ospf 1   #router ospf <process-id>

network 155.238.4.96 0.0.0.15 area 0   #network <network> <wildcard-mask> area <id>

network 155.238.4.208 0.0.0.15 area 0

end

Verifying routing protocol configuration

show ip protocols

Sample output:

Routing Protocol is "ospf 1"

  Outgoing update filter list for all interfaces is not set

  Incoming update filter list for all interfaces is not set

  Router ID 155.238.4.225

  Number of areas in this router is 1. 1 normal 0 stub 0 nssa

  Maximum path: 4

  Routing for Networks:

    155.238.4.96 0.0.0.15 area 0

    155.238.4.208 0.0.0.15 area 0

 Reference bandwidth unit is 100 mbps

  Routing Information Sources:

    Gateway   Distance   Last Update

    155.238.4.225   110   00:15:14

    155.238.4.210   110   00:14:35

  Distance: (default is 110)

4.6. Generating Traffic

IP SLA was used to generate enough UDP traffic between routers which was of equivalent of a live high resolution video stream. With IP SLA, both source and destination devices have to be configured.

Total frame size = Resolution x Bits per pixel (bpp), where resolution is the pixels in *length x width* format.

Using 1080p resolution: Total frame size = (1920x1080)x8

$$= 16588800 \text{ bits/8}$$

$$= 2025 \text{ Kb}$$

Using the command router command *show interface f0/0 #<fast-ethernet> on an enabled router,* a link bandwidth currently set on the router is displayed as output. Therefore current bandwidth was 10Mbps.

According to Wang,K. J. typical packets at low bit rates for the H.264 codec are between 500 – 1500. Therefore 500 packets were chosen as the packet size in this simulation.

4.6.1. Commands to receive traffic at destination:

enable

configure terminal

ip sla responder

exit

4.6.2. Commands to generate traffic at source:

#sending 500 packets every sec with a payload of 2045 b

enable

configure terminal

ip sla 1

udp-jitter 155.238.4.97 13684 num-packets 500

request-data-size 2045

threshold 500

timeout 500

frequency 1

ip sla schedule 1 life forever start-time now

5.Results

Router name	Ports	Protocol
Cape-Town_Campus	f0/0, f1/2	RIP
	f0/1, f1/3	OSPF
Bellville_Campus	f0/0, f0/1, f1/2, f1/3	RIP
		OSPF
Wellington_Campus	f1/2, f1/3	RIP
	f0/1, f0/0	OSPF
Mowbray_Campus	f0/0, f0/1, f1/2, f1/3	RIP
		OSPF
Granger-Bay_Campus	f1/2, f0/1	RIP
	f0/0, f1/3	OSPF

After the routers were all configured, each link connection was captured with Wireshark to validate the configuration and confirm communication between routers by the "Hello" message and the response.

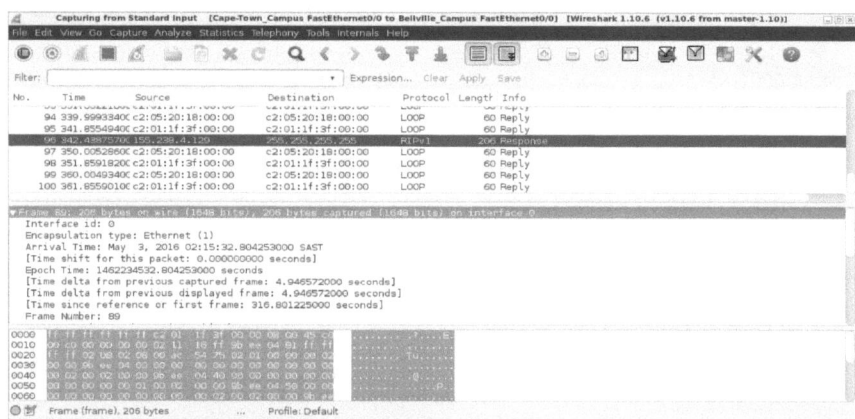

Figure 5.1.   Wireshark RIP capture

The Wireshark capture file above show captured packets for RIP between the Cape-Town_Campus router and the Bellville_Campus router.

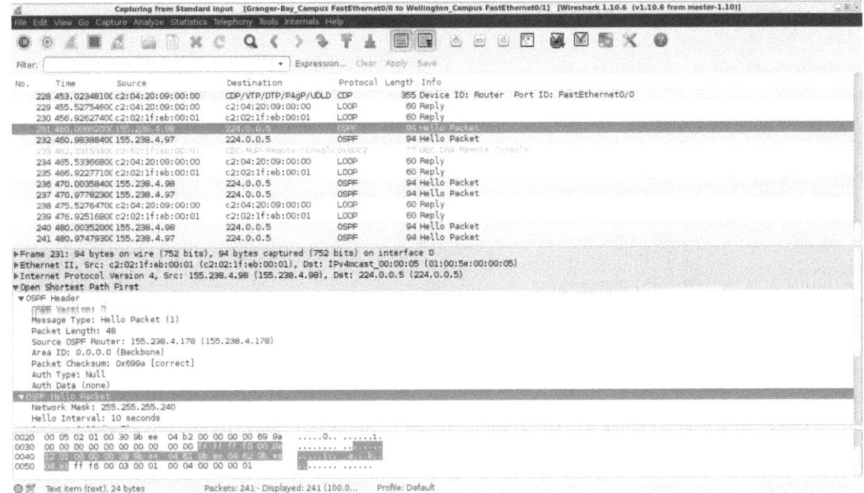

Figure 5.2. Wireshark OSPF capture

As the figure 5.2 indicates, a OSPF configuration between the Granger-Bay_Campus router and the Wellington_Campus router works. Both host are sending out "Hello" packets.

5.1. Capturing traffic

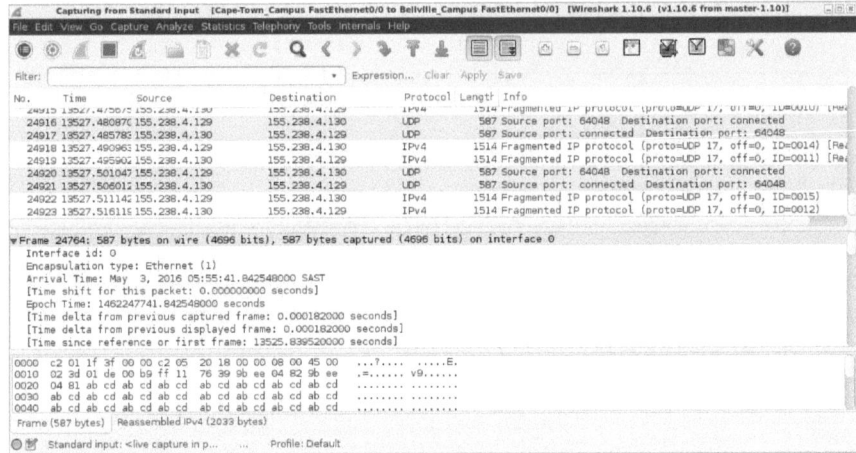

The image above show incoming traffic captured in Wireshark between RIP configured routers.

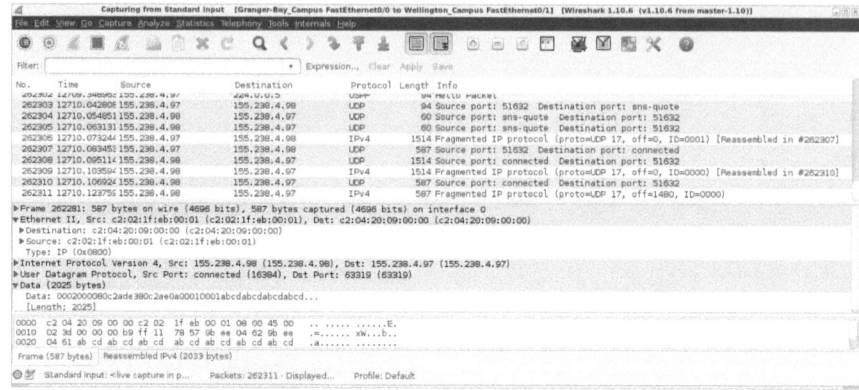

Fugure 5.1.1. Traffic capture

Figure 5.1.1. show incoming traffic on OSPF configure routers.

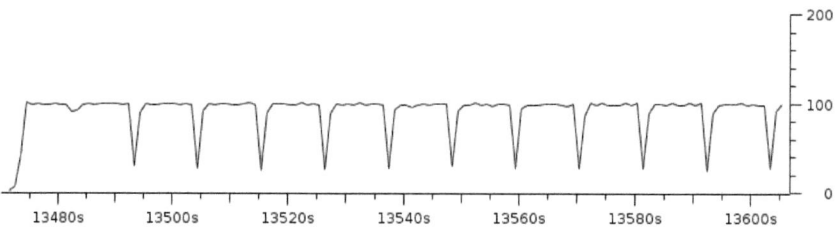

RIP traffic graphical plot showing packets (y-axis)/ time (x-axis):

From the graph above, it seems that RIP has a balance between its end-to-end delay for packets. RIP approximately routes the same amount of packets each time which explains the fact that it is a hop-count routing protocol, the amount of hops would stay the same to reach a destination each time unless there is a broken connection. It show that the jitter is also steady meaning there is no queueing delay on the way to the destination.

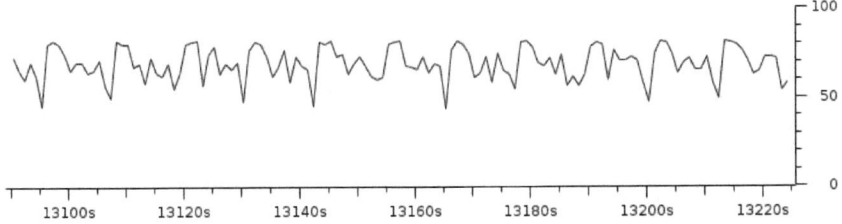

OSPF traffic graphiоal plot showinɡ packets (y-axis)/ time (x-axis):

According to the graph above, OSPF seems to fluctuate on the end-to-end delay. OSPF also takes different size packets each time it routes a packet to a destination. A complete route seems to take ~ 12.5 seconds to reach its destination. The fluctuation of the packet size could make it difficult to determine how long in advance it would take to route a packet.

6.   Conclusion

RIP chooses routes based on hop-counts, whereas OSPF bases it routes on the link itself. From the graphs it showed that RIP is more reliable in terms of steady delays meaning the chances of experiencing unexpected glitches using RIP are slim, however it the opposite with OSPF.

7.   Recommendation

Further simulations could be conducted with other metrics such as different types of communications (fibre optic, coaxial cable and wireless networks).

8.   References

Rosen, E.,*Multiprotocol Label Switching Architecture, Standard Track.,* 2001., Available from: <http://tools.ietf.org/html/rfc3031#page-3>.

Hendrik, C.,*Routing Information Protocol, Network Working Group.*, 1988., Available from: <http://tools.ietf.org/html/rfc1058.html>.

Banks, E., Networking Basics: OSPF Protocol Explained, Auvik., 2014., Available from: <https://www.auvik.com/media/blog/ospf-protocol-explained/>.

Heap, G & Maynes L., *CCNA Practical Studies.,* 2002., Cisco Press., Indianapolis.

Winger, S . , "RTP Payload Format for H.264 Video", RFC 3984, February 2005.

Coded, I., 2003. H.264 compression learn and use in practice!

Pandya, K., 2013. Network Structure or Topology. , 1(2), pp.22–27.

H.264 compression - learn and use in practice!. 2016. *H.264 compression - learn and use in practice!.* [ONLINE] Available at: http://www.dipolnet.com/h_264_compression_-_learn_and_use_in_practice__bib312.htm. [Accessed Marchl 2016].

Videoconferencing Traffic: Network Requirements | Jisc community. 2016. *Videoconferencing Traffic: Network Requirements | Jisc community.* [ONLINE] Available at: https://community.jisc.ac.uk/library/janet-services-documentation/videoconferencing-traffic-network-requirements. [Accessed April 2016].

Nicholas J Humfrey. 2016. *Subnet Mask Cheat Sheet.* [ONLINE] Available at:https://www.aelius.com/njh/subnet_sheet.html. [Accessed April 2016].

Coded, I., 2003. H.264 compression learn and use in practice!

Pandya, K., 2013. Network Structure or Topology. , 1(2), pp.22–27.

9. Appendices

Startup configuration for Cape Town router:

```
!
version 12.4
service timestamps debug datetime msec
service timestamps log datetime msec
no service password-encryption
!
hostname Cape-Town
!
boot-start-marker
boot-end-marker
!
no aaa new-model
memory-size iomem 5
ip cef
multilink bundle-name authenticated
!
archive
 log config
  hidekeys
!
vlan internal allocation policy ascending
!
interface FastEthernet0/0
 ip address 155.238.4.130 255.255.255.240
 duplex auto
 speed auto
!
interface FastEthernet0/1
 ip address 155.238.4.113 255.255.255.240
 duplex auto
 speed auto
!
interface FastEthernet1/0
 no switchport
```

```
 ip address 155.238.4.49 255.255.255.240
!
interface FastEthernet1/1
!
interface FastEthernet1/2
 no switchport
 ip address 155.238.4.194 255.255.255.240
!
interface FastEthernet1/3
 no switchport
 ip address 155.238.4.210 255.255.255.240
!
interface FastEthernet1/4
!
interface FastEthernet1/5
!
interface FastEthernet1/6
!
interface FastEthernet1/7
!

!
interface Vlan1
 no ip address
!
router ospf 1
 log-adjacency-changes
 network 155.238.4.112 0.0.0.15 area 0
 network 155.238.4.208 0.0.0.15 area 0
!
ip forward-protocol nd
!
!
no ip http server
no ip http secure-server
!
ip sla responder
!
!
```

```
!
control-plane
!
line con 0
line aux 0
line vty 0 4
 login
!
!
end
```

Startup configuration for Granger-Bay router:

```
!
version 12.4
service timestamps debug datetime msec
service timestamps log datetime msec
no service password-encryption
!
hostname Granger-Bay
!
boot-start-marker
boot-end-marker
!
!
no aaa new-model
memory-size iomem 5
!
ip traffic-export profile gbc
  interface FastEthernet0/0
  bidirectional
  mac-address c202.1feb.0000
ip cef
!
multilink bundle-name authenticated
!
archive
 log config
  hidekeys
!
```

```
vlan internal allocation policy ascending
!
interface FastEthernet0/0
 ip address 155.238.4.97 255.255.255.240
 ip traffic-export apply gbc
 duplex auto
 speed auto
!
interface FastEthernet0/1
 ip address 155.238.4.82 255.255.255.240
 duplex auto
 speed auto
!
interface FastEthernet1/0
 no switchport
 ip address 155.238.4.17 255.255.255.240
!
interface FastEthernet1/1
!
interface FastEthernet1/2
 no switchport
 ip address 155.238.4.225 255.255.255.240
!
interface FastEthernet1/3
 no switchport
 ip address 155.238.4.209 255.255.255.240
!
interface FastEthernet1/4
!
interface Vlan1
 no ip address
!
router ospf 1
 log-adjacency-changes
 network 155.238.4.96 0.0.0.15 area 0
 network 155.238.4.208 0.0.0.15 area 0
!
ip forward-protocol nd
!
```

```
!
no ip http server
no ip http secure-server
!
ip sla logging traps
ip sla 1
 udp-jitter 155.238.4.98 16384 num-packets 500
 request-data-size 2025
 timeout 500
 threshold 500
 frequency 1
ip sla schedule 1 life forever start-time now
!
control-plane
!
line con 0
line aux 0
line vty 0 4
 login
!
end
```